a kiss

for the worthy

Poetry inspired by the Walt Whitman
poem 'Leaves of Grass'

*A Love Poetry Trilogy
Book 2*

Frank Prem

Publication Details

Published by Wild Arancini Press
Copyright © 2020 Frank Prem

All rights reserved:
No part of this publication may be reproduced, stored in a retrieval system, or transmitted in any form or by any means, electronic, mechanical, photocopying, recording or otherwise, without prior written permission from the publisher and author.

Title: *a kiss for the worthy*
ISBN 978-1-925963-04-5 (pbk)
ISBN 978-1-925963-05-2 (e-bk)

This collection is dedicated to the world we live in.

How we are tolerated, only heaven can knows.

Contents

about a love poetry trilogy	1
Song of Myself (Leaves of Grass)	2
a kiss for the worthy part 1	5
mmm-hmmm (this day)	7
see then sing (then rise)	9
in the midst I cannot think	11
is beautiful (this year)	13
much like the bees (with your permission)	15
a kiss (for the worthy)	17
atomically speaking	18
clean (this soil, my air)	20
born here (an immigrant son)	22
soft warnings	25
not until (I die)	27
wisdom (but only small)	29
sufficient (at the heart)	31
a singing part (of me)	33
in blossom wild (a nature boy)	35
a kiss for the worthy part 2	37
a house filled (with the sensual)	39
what I am (a lapwing's call)	41
every (working) man	43
espresso (no and no)	45
here (and there)	48
chance encounter (with a lasting liquor)	50
simply (forever) sensory	52
the day (by the bank in the wood) does what it may wish	54
not much left (of me)	56
only I	58
two air (one)	60
and why	62
which way (sustained)	64

better because	66
the need to test (for life)	68
inhale (my heart)	71
a stone (a shell)	73
bad wind (upon your eddies)	75
be this (with kisses)	77
the benevolence (plays)	78
baylis street (in a rush)	80
unseasonably (I wander)	81
being (the herald)	83
of day and of rising (to a song)	85
the original project	87
source materials	89
author information	91
other published works	93
what readers say	95
coming soon	101

about

a love poetry trilogy

A Kiss For The Worthy is the second of three poetry collections written for *A Love Poetry Trilogy*.

The origin of this work goes back a number of years to an occasion when I was fortunate to participate in a project that involved individual poets located around the globe.

Each poet chose a phrase from the body of a distinguished poem written long in the past, and used that phrase as inspiration for a piece of new poetry. New and old were then hyperlinked together to create an interactive work.

Over the course of the project, three poems (and their poets) were chosen as source material for the experiment:

Amy Lowell – *Madonna of the Evening Flowers* (1919)
Walt Whitman – *Leaves of Grass* (1855) Parts 1 and 2 (1855)
T.S. Eliot - *The Love Song of J. Alfred Prufrock* (1915) (Epigraph plus Stanzas 1 – 5)

To the best of my knowledge, no trace remains of the original project, but I was recently inspired to revisit and to continue an exploration of the effects these wonderful poems might have on my own work.

Each source poem commanded its own identifiable voice in my responses, and here I have worked with the Whitman poem.

It is a vast piece of poetry that Whitman spent much of his lifetime revising and rewriting and republishing. The relevant extract follows.

Song of Myself (Leaves of Grass)

1

I CELEBRATE myself, and sing myself,
And what I assume you shall assume,
For every atom belonging to me as good belongs to you.

I loafe and invite my soul,
I lean and loafe at my ease observing a spear of summer grass.

My tongue, every atom of my blood, form'd from this soil, this air,
Born here of parents born here from parents the same, and their parents the same,
I, now thirty-seven years old in perfect health begin,
Hoping to cease not till death.

Creeds and schools in abeyance,
Retiring back a while sufficed at what they are, but never forgotten,
I harbor for good or bad, I permit to speak at every hazard,
Nature without check with original energy.

2

Houses and rooms are full of perfumes, the shelves are crowded with perfumes,
I breathe the fragrance myself and know it and like it,
The distillation would intoxicate me also, but I shall not let it.

The atmosphere is not a perfume, it has no taste of the distillation, it is odorless,
It is for my mouth forever, I am in love with it,
I will go to the bank by the wood and become undisguised and naked,
I am mad for it to be in contact with me.

The smoke of my own breath,
Echoes, ripples, buzz'd whispers, love-root, silk-thread, crotch and vine,
My respiration and inspiration, the beating of my heart, the pass-ing of blood and air through my lungs,
The sniff of green leaves and dry leaves, and of the shore and dark-color'd sea-rocks, and of hay in the barn,
The sound of the belch'd words of my voice loos'd to the eddies of the wind,
A few light kisses, a few embraces, a reaching around of arms,
The play of shine and shade on the trees as the supple boughs wag,
The delight alone or in the rush of the streets, or along the fields and hill-sides,
The feeling of health, the full-noon trill, the song of me rising from bed and meeting the sun.

Walt Whitman – 1855

a kiss for the worthy
part 1

mmm-hmmm (this day)

I CELEBRATE myself, and sing myself

and here I am
the morning come

I rise again
I rise

the sun serves
to illuminate
this world of mine

I rise to kiss
the light

ray
by ray
and beam
by shining beam

I sing
to myself
a satisfaction
for the knowledge
that I *am*

for the *being*
that is me

I laugh
a little dance
as though a stream
a rill
across the smoothing stones
of the woolshed creek

phwee
phwee-phwee
phwee phwee

I whistle to myself
oh
how I love the day

and how
I love
this day

phwee
phwee-phwee
phwee
phwee

mmm-hmmm

see then sing (then rise)

And what I assume you shall assume

I
will sing songs
as though
the heavens sang

open up
my voice
with great
conviction

and I
will sing
for you

croon
my love of
being
beneath
a southern sky

let you hear
my heart

its rhythm
beating
beating

beating

and you will see
what I see
through the tenor
of my tones
assume
what I assume
is right
within the song

it is
of a dry
and blue
wide heaven
that I sing

of constellations
that populate the night

the southern cross
and
the pointer

so sing with me

come
sing with me

let us
be
our voices

and rise

note
by note

above ourselves

beyond

in the midst I cannot think

For every atom belonging to me as good belongs to you

it is
difficult

to think

in the presence
of my own
self

there are times
when I . . .

the very *fact*
of me
becomes
overwhelming

it is the awareness
of *being*

the knowledge that
I

am

my thought
is comprised

compromised

by every atom
belonging to me

establishing *me*
in my own awareness
in such a way that
nothing

no-thing

and
no-*other*-one

is established

what glory
is this

what joy

what knowledge

who
can think
while in the midst

the very midst

of their own
being

is beautiful (this year)

I loafe and invite my soul

I will wander
wool gathering
in my mind

as the wind
blows
stray petals of white blossom
shed by the generosity
of the golden plum
before me

a loaf along

my face
to a breeze
that brings the power
of fragrance

the fresh flowers
of spring

and I
invite my soul
to join me

sing
a sabbatical
pastorale

including
the fleeting flash
of red
and the squeaking pitch
of rosellas
shrilly arguing
in waking branches
of the sentinel oak

what better wool
than this
to gather

what better awareness
of spring

could there be anything
better
than to *be*
residing
as one
with my soul

the pink
of the peach
is beautiful
this year

much like the bees (with your permission)

I lean and loafe at my ease

end of winter

a balmy day

you
sitting in the sun
while I lean

casual

at my ease

watching

bees
are at the blossom
already

the season
will not wait

and your permission
to clear
the garden boxes
becomes a vision
of clarity

to be asserted
where tangles now grow
in obfuscation

I envisage
a time
not long away

of secateurs
and shears
and shovels

happy work
much like the bees
and blooms

but
today
I lean

and contemplate

completely
at my
ease

a kiss (for the worthy)

Observing a spear of summer grass

the susurrations sing
to their gentling
by a breeze

blown a kiss
through
the unbending
spikelets
of chocolate coloured
bulrush flowers

ripened
and waiting to cast seed
into the care
of that fleeting grace

is that not
a tune
worthy of singing

worthy
of a kiss
from zephyr
passing by

atomically speaking

> *My tongue, every atom of my blood*

I speak aloud

speak
with passion
in each utterance

I speak to you

tell you
everything
I
believe in

I talk
to the night as well
and speak aloud
your name

my tongue
finds the way to say
you

with all of me
entwined
within that word

spoken to you
my words
take
new meanings

with you
listening
what I say
holds
new worth

and I say it
again

say it
aloud

I say it
to you

clean (this soil, my air)

Form'd from this soil, this air

too long
have I
neglected

too few the times
my hand
has reached
to smooth the soil

I know my soul
seeks balm
and know
where
I should seek it

but . . .

so often
my gaze is distorted
through the bending
of a rippled pane

and so often
I wish that I could see
a proof

evidence
of my own making

a boot print
and a thing
of green
and growing

succour for a heart
rising
right from this soil
of mine

breathing my own air

releasing me

to be
again
full cleansed

born here (an immigrant son)

Born here of parents born here from parents the same, and their parents the same

I come
from a long line
of strangers

born
of here

born
of this

my parents
born
somewhere away
are both
of here
just the same

and theirs before

and theirs
before

came over mountains
crossed
the wilding seas

and they flew
in an airplane

so strange

but
feet on this ground
they were landed
beneath the heavens

here

into this place
where their lives
new
began

so
sing me a song
of an immigrant
on the road

sing me the song
of a traveller

I will join you
in the chorus
for I carry
that same dusty weight

let us sing
and then be
gone

like the wind
away

I come
from a line
so long
of *strangers*
once

they were strangers
born to be
as one
with *this*
their place

as I
am born to be one
with it

and with this road
that winds

as
it ever
has

soft warnings

I, now thirty-seven years old in perfect health begin

I
once thirty-seven years
and perfect health
was a man

such a man

I was
everything
and every thing
was begun

by me

for me

because
of who and what
I was

I thought myself
so fine

thought myself
so very fine

for I could not conceive
of a thing
that would not
fall
at my feet
when I desired it

thirty-seven
once
I was

everything of me
begun

who could see
and who
could say

that the shimmer
was only
a mirage

a life
equal only
to the swaying
of an illusion

beliefs . . .

a mirage

I look
at thirty-seven
now
and I look beyond
for thirty-six

to whisper
warnings

I whisper
my thirty-six
soft warnings

not until (I die)

Hoping to cease not till death

and
while I breathe
this
clear
honeyed air

while I can taste
the flavours
of a day

this day

my day

I can see I can touch
feel
and hear

I
can inhale

the aroma
that is life

my life

.
.
.

alive

I am alive

and it is so
very good
this ambrosia
of breathing

of being . . .

me

may I go on
and on

and
may I last

each breath in me

hoping
never to cease

not
until I die

wisdom (but only small)

Creeds and schools in abeyance

and here
I consider for myself
my own inclination
to utterance

what I think

what I
believe

my
leanings

all those things
as yet
by me
unspoken

thoughts
that I choose
not
as yet
to share in words

aloud

they
may bide their time

may wait
for a different
audience

perhaps
I will never let them fly
released
to drift
among the spoken airs

who am I
after all
to speak
my
every passing thought

who am I
to believe
those thoughts
have even
some
small claim

mine is not
a lofty mind

I . . .

am
a poor specimen

raised
from nothing very much
to be . . .

nothing
so very much

and yet

and so

I believe it
wise
with my small allocation
of humility
to keep them

safely

in abeyance

sufficient (at the heart)

Retiring back a while sufficed at what they are, but never forgotten

it is not necess . . .

I mean
don't feel you always mus . . .

come
back here
where I am

it is not
always required
that you take
the lead

sometimes
the mob may run
before you

sometimes
the action seems
up there
way ahead

away ahead

but here
is where you are

here
is your
entire world
(this moment)

be at peace
for you suffice
you know

wherever you are
in the teeming
you suffice

and sometimes
you may be unremembered

so it seems
so
it seems

but the heart
of the universe
does not forget
you

always it spins
around
where you stand

so stride
large footsteps
or small

stride out
across the story
of your life

with you
yourself
at the heart
of things

as it should be

you
sufficient
unto yourself

a singing part (of me)

I harbor for good or bad, I permit to speak at every hazard

I watch
a tiny speck
high up in the sky
harassing an eagle

so much ferocity
in one
so small

there is no love
lost
between the hunter
and its prey

but the eagle
is just another bird

its rapt attention
given
to the whole
of each day

there is no good
in it

no bad

and no matter what
may come
the day remains

my love
is for the eagle
for the shape
of it

the grace

and I love
the magpie
for the chortling
of its song

even though
the one
may exact
an existential toll

I keep the song
alive

just as I feel
the day
is alive

I keep it
singing

a part of me

in blossom wild (a nature boy)

Nature without check with original energy

nature boy

creature
of flowers

meadow dancer

yellow
among the daisy
everlastings
and
the growing wild

rumpled
by a breeze unchecked

and blowing . . .

blowing
with all the energy
of a nature boy

forest child

and fauna
that you are

snuffling
and sneezing

the flower
of a blue-gum tree
is the place
you live

a nature boy
in blossom

wild

a kiss for the worthy

part 2

a house filled (with the sensual)

Houses and rooms are full of perfumes

I watch them
in the early morning
hours

they are closed
before the sun

like
little rooms
little houses
un-obtruding
on the lawn

waiting for
daylight proper

and as they open
I realise
they are filled
with sweet perfumes

golden glory

wafted aroma

released now
to attract the buzz
of business

the bees come

they must

and the shape of this
unfolding
day
is revealed

there is pollen
there is
nectar
there is humming
in the air

happy work
and happy
the sensual wafting
of a siren call

the lazy
drift
of sweet perfume

until
the sun wanders
westward

the scent
of ready lust
is withdrawn

little rooms
into
little houses

until tomorrow

gone

what I am (a lapwing's call)

The shelves are crowded with perfumes

I enumerate
the birds
that fill my yard

some days
there is no room
for a man
to walk

for there are ibis
and bower

blackbird

king
and
rosella

silver eye

the wattle-o
with his fire flash
of red
dangled flesh
as an angry declaration
and a look
cast
from a pollen-maddened eye

black and white chortlers
sing
to properly declare
the day

the jackass
laughs
at the evening

and the lapwings
call
a screech of love
in the dead
of night

I take them in

take
all of them
right in

inhale them
as though
they are the scent
that makes me
what I am

every (working) man

I breathe the fragrance myself and know it and like it

and it is
glorious

the sun
warming
across my bent back

and it is
wonderful

the feeling
of this body
working

sweat
on my brow
sweat
rolling down my chest

down my arms

the beauty of a man
at toil

my perspiration
is evaporating
in ripple waves

I breathe
the fragrance of myself
and today
I like it

I am
the working version
of myself
this day

and I am mighty

with bare arms
or spade or axe

I know
this
is a kind
of beauty

I know it is only
because
of what I do

myself

everyman

every working man

I inhale this day
of work
once again
and I like it

I so
do like it

espresso (no and no)

The distillation would intoxicate me also, but I shall not let it

I cannot drink
this beverage
anymore

although
it is right here
by my hand

and right by
the desire
of my heart

I take the beans
that come from
jamaica

beans
that come to me
from india
from senegal
from
I do not know where

but I take them
with their sour smell
of green
and roast them

always turning

always turning them
toward
the brown

heating
until I hear
their song

a percussive tune
of click
on click

of crackling
in the pan

until the sour
is a faded memory
and the aroma
itself
can move the heart

I draw it in

I draw it in

a distillation
that could intoxicate me
were I a weaker being

but
I shall not let it

I know
three cups
is just not right

not right
at all
but
the first cup
is such a pleasure

the second
just happens
somehow . . .

I don't know

a third cup
of this divine transport
would leave me . . .

would take me . . .

I might wake up
still flying
but
more likely
crashed
and burned

I do not care
so much
for rehabilitation

it is a dull
and flavourless
pastime

so
I will be strong
right now
and say no

to my waiting
espresso machine

no
to the beans
I have already ground
(somehow
when I was not attentive)

no
to another
short one
and sharp

no
I will put the coffee
down

here (and there)

The atmosphere is not a perfume

it does not need
to be
a mountain

or the very top
of the tallest
of the poplars
in the township

such locations are
evocative
but the *idea* of them
is enough
to be
my transport

I look to the height
of an oak tree
inhabitant of my back yard
these eighty years

longer
perhaps

the contemplation
is enough

I am there

I am the magpie
perched
on the highest slender branch

swaying

and the atmosphere
I know
is only air
and not perfume
but
it is intoxicating
to me

I close my mouth
and inhale
loud
and deep

it is
the whole earth
that I breathe

risen from the ground

the dirt
the grass

the salt
of a distant sea

I take it in

the top
of my mountain

the tip branch
of my tree

I take it in

I am there
and . . .

and
I
am here

chance encounter (with a lasting liquor)

It has no taste of the distillation, it is odorless

there is
no taste
to this

there is no
odour

there is only
the *I*
of me

the *eau*
of a being

distilled
from what I am
it is
sufficient

the sensation on your lips
is the taste
of a man
alive

and I
bestride
your rapid
thought-ways

I walk
I march
along your covered paths

places
you thought safe
that
you thought
hidden

I will shelter there
for a night
leave my touch
and then
go

for I am
the day

I am the night time

I am the light that shines
on you
to confirm
you live

yes
you live

when I am gone
the daze
will be left

the drunkenness
of *is*
the nevermore
of *was*

odourless
and tasteless
it shall be
you
distilled

remaining
for all time

simply (forever) sensory

It is for my mouth forever, I am in love with it

and I take
the morning

take the rising sun

the new light
and the feeling of dew
still
in the air

I take it in
with my eyes

my ears
hold on to the sounds

and I taste it

this day

another day

who could believe
such luck
and
such wonder

it is in my mouth now
and will be there
forever

oh day

the breath of you
deep
in my lungs

A KISS FOR THE WORTHY

I stand here
and know
what I love

I love
forever

the day (by the bank in the wood) does what it may wish

I will go to the bank by the wood

and is it not
at times
such as these

such trying times as these
that the need
to *be*
emerges

times like these
for *self*
to finally
fully
emerge

on a day of depths
and darkness
before the light
wander
by the embankment

to the secluded place
along the old railway line
in and among
the eucalypts

go there
as you are

your own self

for
who else should you be
on such a day
in such a time
as this

how else can you tell
if this is really
you

strip your clothes
down to the flesh

beyond

strip yourself
until you see
a fleeting glimpse
of what is
your spirit

this . . .

this will be
a day
so like
unlike
any other

and you
will stand still
while it does
what it needs to do

does to you
whatever
it may wish

not much left (of me)

And become undisguised and naked

strip me back
flay
my skin

suspend it
on a low-hung wire

take the meat
away
from the skeleton

weigh
each ingredient
essential

rattle all the bones

there is not much else
that is left
of me

what I
was and
what
I am
and what
I will be

what do you see
when you look
through me

animate my skin
make me dance
all my flesh in a pile
beside me

bones
beating loud
like a drum upon the cavity
of my heart

sending a signal
that

I am
naked

I am undisguised

what you see
are portions
and pieces

traces

of what I was

and that is all
(that is all)
that I
can be

only I

I am mad for it to be in contact with me

heady stuff
the world I breathe

I take in colour
from the leaves

I take in
grey
and white

I absorb the sun

wave
in the breeze

sway

headiness
in contact
with myself

an atmosphere
swooping low
all
around me

I am mad
for it

I am wild
to touch each particle
that motes
the sky

that is *mine*

only *I*
can see it

touch it

only *I*
can breathe it

smell the aroma
of this day

heady stuff

for only
I

two air (one)

The smoke of my own breath

in the evening
our game
is to intertwine

arms
and legs
as we walk

breath directed
on the diagonal

from my mouth
and lips
to intersect
the soft mist
of breath
from your
mouth and lips

we laugh
at the mingling

your breath
with mine
and mine as one
with yours

we are like two smokers
sharing
what we inhale

after changing it
inside ourselves

to make it your breath
of mist

my breath
of smoke

our air

one

and why

Echoes, ripples, buzz'd whispers

echoes
ripples
those buzzed whispers

caressing
inside my mind

tell me . . .

they are telling me . . .

sometimes . . .

I don't know
what they say

but the message
is an urgency

I feel it
exactly
that way

what will
tomorrow
bring

I wonder
but
I don't know

buzzed whispers
echo

.
  .
    .

and tell

reveal themselves
in time

show both
answer
and
why

which way (sustained)

Love-root, silk-thread, crotch and vine

I approach
with ultimate
trepidation

ultimate desire

silken threads
run
from me
to . . .

to . . .

what
I wonder

where

down which fork
will I
be drawn

from death
feeling my way
toward
life

toward light

or
do I go
deeper

ever deeper

the love root
is there

bathed
in the light

here
in the darkness
it is only myself

only the *I*
that is changed

which way
do I go

better because

My respiration and inspiration, the beating of my heart

into each
of my contemplations
I place
my heart

the beating
of my heart

to enter thought
requires
the whole of me

or so I believe

so
I believe

with every breath
a new insight

the more I breathe
the more
I know

and so
on twenty-three thousand
occasions
each and every day

I throw myself
the full length
of myself
within

and so
my knowledge grows
and it inspires

twenty-three thousand
times
I find my way
toward light

even now
as I ponder at my ease
this way of thought
is new

and I am more

a bigger
better man
now
because I know

I am more than me
because

I know

the need to test (for life)

The pass-ing of blood and air through my lungs

the feeling of life
that comes
with the first rays
of the sun

when I wake up
to the day

the passing cool
of air
filling up my lungs

of blood pumped
around
by my beating heart

I know:

I am aware

I know:

I am thinking

and so
I am alive

how could I be
alive
if I did not
really know

sometimes
I need to pinch
myself
to feel the pain

watch
the bloodless whiteness
then
the red

sometimes I speak my
ouch
aloud
just to hear

just
for the sound
of my voice

the little confirmations
and small certainties
available
to be tested

after the night

after
every night

when I
might have died
for all that I know

.
.
.

I wonder
sometimes
how much proof
would prove to be
enough

but
how can I stop

when
is that point
when I no longer need
to know

forgive me
I am tedious
I believe I may have
a small obsession

but the moment
that I stop
is the moment
I no longer know
and truly
I wonder

how
can I be
sure
that I am really
alive

if not
by testing

inhale (my heart)

The sniff of green leaves and dry leaves, and of the shore

I strode the sands
once
of the chelsea
shoreline

walked
through the wavelets
on hampton beach

and where I strode
I raised
the salt flecks
in froth
and in the bubbles

to splash
in the shallows
for me . . .

it was
sublime

but in my heart
I retained
the leaves

the smell of eucalyptus
both dry
and green

I am overwhelmed
by their aroma
when walking
through forest

and I believe
that is where
my heart resides

so I hold
the memories
of salt
inside me

all those times
of white spray
to recall

but I run my feet
through the leaves
at the base
of the woodland

crush
a green leaf

my heart
inhale

a stone (a shell)

And dark-color'd sea-rocks, and of hay in the barn

I keep
on the ledge
in my house
a stone
and a shell

took them
both
from the sea
at lowest water

I left
an exchange

my own footprints
bedded
within the sand

until the tide
swept in
to shore

and I glance
sometimes
at my small
sea stone

dip it
below
an inch of water

to watch the darkness
steal across
yet
make clean

I am a man
of fields
and grasses

my purpose
lies alongside hay
stored
and under cover

my hands
are rough

utility's weapons

and no amount
of water
can make them
gleam

but I recall
a day

one day
of seaside

I recall
the imprint I made
with my naked feet

I left some part
of myself
in that caress
by soft sand

took a stone
and
a shell

for the mark
of me

bad wind (upon your eddies)

The sound of the belch'd words of my voice loos'd to the eddies of the wind

so I stand
to speak

I know that you
can hear me

I know the way my voice
the gout of belching words I utter
and let loose
upon the winds
affects you

fails
to affect you

but

here I stand
and I
will speak

again

I will tell you
of what I know

of what I believe

I will tell
what *is*
the truth of the matter

I will shout
at you
the truth
of the matter

stamp my feet
until I fear
(I hope)
the earth
the very earth
will tremble beneath you

but you

ha

you
I know
are stoppered

aurally insulated
to filter out
the lesser words

the undesirable

the provocative

and yet
I belch at you
for my world

the world that I
so love

the only world
I can ever know
is burning to ash
in my mouth

released to float
as flecks of grey
blown
in lazy swirling eddies
by your winds

be this (with kisses)

A few light kisses, a few embraces, a reaching around of arms

close your eyes

close them
I say

turn your face
up
to feel the sun
pouring
warm and light
and good
upon it

a benison and boon
that is its own reward
for being

spread wide
your arms

feel the breeze
embrace you
surround you
with light kisses
placed
as small reminders
of life
that tingle you
at their touch

spread your arms wide

your eyes closed

be them

be
this

the benevolence (plays)

The play of shine and shade on the trees as the supple boughs wag

by day I watch
the play of shine
and shade

deciduous twins
that dominate my seasons

how tall is tall

how wide

enough
to be a new atmosphere
when standing
beneath
the leaves

enough to be called home
by the trillers
and warblers
that fill each day

enough
and supple
to reach

to reach toward
the sky

boughs and branches
wag
swaying to a song
sung in gentled whispers
by
the benevolence

the breeze

they are
the leafed instrument
for all the day
to play

baylis street (in a rush)

The delight alone or in the rush of the streets

I wander
streets

as though
I have never wandered
before

these pavements
have the feeling
of *new*
to my feet

treading lightly
with a buoyancy
of delight
that is itself
a rush of sensation

for new streets
are like . . .

in a small way
are like
new planets
where even the atmosphere
must be learned
before the commencement
of true breathing

I could dance
or skip
heels clicking in the air

for the joy
of the new

on these streets I am
in a way
reborn

unseasonably (I wander)

Or along the fields and hill-sides

it is my mind
that does the wandering
not I

I remain
upholstered
in my easy chair

I gaze
unseasonably
at the fire

while my mind
sends reports
in an image stream

a *show*
without
a *tell*

a transportation
enabled
by the dance
of flames

I remember
a murmungee hill-side

a slope
that I perched above

a fog below
that covered
the fields
to make what I saw

a cloud scape

thick enough
that I could
perhaps
step upon it

like a man
crossing water

I feel again
that touch of sun
when I raised my face

closed my eyes

as I close my eyes
now
to feel the fire glow

unseasonably
that kind
of warm

being (the herald)

The feeling of health, the full-noon trill

I rise up

comes the dawn

it heralds me
I
herald the day

and as the grey
retreats
and the green enlivens

the sun shines golden
new light

there is a feeling
of wellness

of health
that is the cycle
of being
once again

and I sing
with a warbling magpie
still learning
the noon day trill

we sing along
with each other

and between us two
the day must know
that it is being

that *we*
are being

and that
heralds the best feeling
that I know

of day and of rising (to a song)

The song of me rising from bed and meeting the sun

it is a soundless
song

sung by
sensation

sung
by touch

I hear it
before
I open up my eyes

I hear it
through an alteration
in my awareness

I hear it call me
awake

awake

it is time
to rise

and I find
my feet
have migrated
to the floor
below

suddenly
I am standing

called
to face the window

called to sight the filtered light
streaming in
through veiled curtains

I pull them aside

the song
grows louder now

and inside
I am singing

meet the sun

I
meet the sun

this song
of day

the original project

My initial response and submission (written for the project around 2001) was the poem *the atmosphere is not a perfume* which I have included below. It will be easy for a reader to identify it as work from an earlier phase of my writing career.

the atmosphere is not a perfume

The atmosphere is not a perfume

this atmosphere is not a perfume
but is the presence that still remains
in contours shaped when you rose to leave
with morning

I am embracing the slow escape of warmth
to find comfort in this chilling room
making your image in
the smoke of my own breath
and half day-dreaming

what I cannot do is hold you
grasp as I might to catch the illusion
there is nothing but the trace
left in a tepid fold of cloth
that holds a whisper of the smell of you
and it is my skin that lies alone
bare against the sheets
and last desire

source materials

If you would like to find some information about Walt Whitman, his life and his writing, a good place to start is his entry in Wikipedia: https://en.wikipedia.org/wiki/Walt_Whitman.

I have accessed the source poems for this project from the following online locations:

The Reader (Lowell): https://www.thereader.org.uk/featured-poem-madonna-of-the-evening-flowers-by-amy-lowell/

The Walt Whitman Archive (Whitman): https://whitmanarchive.org/published/LG/

The Poetry Foundation (T. S. Eliot): https://www.poetryfoundation.org/poetrymagazine/poems/44212/the-love-song-of-j-alfred-prufrock

I commend these organisations, and the work of the selected poets to you.

FP
2020

author information

About Frank Prem

Frank Prem has been a storytelling poet since his teenage years. He has been a psychiatric nurse through all of his professional career, which now exceeds forty years.

He has been published in magazines, online zines and anthologies in Australia, and in a number of other countries, and has both performed and recorded his work as spoken word.

He lives with his wife in the beautiful township of Beechworth in North East Victoria, Australia.

Did you enjoy this book?

If you have enjoyed reading *A Kiss for the Worthy*, please take a moment to do two small things.

First, leave a short review of this book on Amazon by visiting **https://mybook.to/A_kiss_for_the_worthy** and clicking on the button (near the bottom of the page) that is labelled "Write a customer review."

Online reviews provide social proof to readers and are critical to Indie authors such as myself.

The second thing is, please visit Frank Prem's webpage at **https://FrankPrem.com** and sign up to join his Newsletter list. From time to time the Newsletter will let you know what is happening with Frank and his writing, as well as keeping you informed of any giveaways that might be planned.

Linkages to other writing and storytelling activities (such as YouTube videos) can be accessed from the Webpage

other published works

Frank Prem

Small Town Kid (2018)
ISBN: 978-0-9751442-3-7 (pbk)
ISBN: 978-0-9751442-4-4 (e-bk)

Devil In The Wind (2019)
ISBN: 978-0-9751442-6-8 (pbk)
ISBN: 978-0-9751442-7-5 (e-bk)

The New Asylum (2019)
ISBN: 978-0-9751442-8-2 (pbk)
ISBN: 978-0-9751442-5-1

With Other Authors

Herja, Devastation - With Cage Dunn (2019)
ISBN: 978-1-925905-04-5 (pbk)
ISBN: 978-1-925905-03-8 (e-bk)

Short Stories of Forest and Fantasy: Fantasy Anthology by OzTales(2019)
ISBN: 978-0-9872863-7-6 (pbk)
ISBN: 978-0-9872863-5-2 (e-bk)

Aquarius: Speculative Fiction Inspired by the Zodiac (The Zodiac Series) by Deadset Press
ISBN: 978-1393586371 (pbk)

what readers say

Small Town Kid

A modern-day minstrel

As a 'New Australian' of eastern European heritage, much of Frenki's life resonates with me, and yet it's the imagery of time and place that makes these poems familiar to all Australians. And perhaps to non-Australians as well. Boyhood and the wonder years. Some things are universal. Highly recommended

—A. F. (Australia)

Small-Town Kid is a wonderful collection
With so few words Frank is able to paint a picture so vivid you can't help but get lost in the story. Whether he's talking about family, a picnic, a trip to the butcher or even the outside toilet it's difficult not become immersed in the words and imagine yourself right there with him. Cover to cover, this is an excellent read.

—S. T. (Australia)

A poet's walk through his childhood in a small Australian town. From the dedication poem, 'I Can Hardly Wait to Show You', to 'Circular Square Town', Frank Prem's chronological journey from infancy to the present has a familiar feel to it, almost as if you were taking a walk through your own memory lane to recall the innumerable small, but unforgettable moments that make up a life.

—J. L. (USA)

Devil In The Wind

I live in the US, and though I recall these fires, I never knew the personal stories behind them. Frank Prem instantly grips you by the throat in his step-by-step story of survival.
I was especially taken because he told the story through poetry, which I've never related to this way. It was stark and vivid, the language of a survivor. It's a quick read, but trust me, this book will stay with you.

Bravo!

—K. K. (USA)

Very moving, beautiful, and terrible

—J. S. (South Africa)

Outstanding!
I'm not normally a reader of poetry, but Devil in the Wind captured the essence of 7 February 2009, and the days and weeks afterwards, with eloquence and ease. Beautifully written, the author has given a human voice to those who matter. Highly recommended.

—B. T. (Australia)

The New Asylum

Brilliant succinct memoir. These insightful, thought provoking behind-the-scene stories are woven so seamlessly you'll lose track of time. 'this somebody's boy' is one of many which will hold your heart.

__M.P-B. (Australia)

Words can't do justice to the emotional journey I travelled in (reading this collection). I don't think anything can. My heart bled, my eyes burned. And I will read it again, to remind me.

__C. D. (Australia)

"The eternal asylums of mental health ...another shift in the backwards."
If I had to pick one book over the past year that has truly resonated with me, this would be it. It's a hauntingly beautiful window into the successes and failures of working with the mentally disabled, and the impact on the human psyche. ( )

__K. B. (USA)

Herja, Devastation

How does a reader give this work the credit it deserves? Simply written, powerfully felt. A man with a job, a woman he loves beyond sanity (or is it his only hold on sanity?).
He is her tool, he says, and I feel the depth of that longing to be nothing more than that. Loved it. Can't say that enough.

__C. (Australia)

The cover alone was enough to excite me to look inside. I'm glad I did.
I loved this book. I don't know whether to call it poetry or prose, and I'd never heard of Eddic tales, but if that's your thing, or you want to feel the subtle menace, albeit from a loving hand.
This is a book I will reread and remember for a long, long time.

__C. (Australia)

As a combination of poetry, prose, and wonderfully ominous illustrations, I found Herja, Devastation refreshingly original. The narrative slipped seamlessly between the two forms and the valkyrie/assassin story carried my interest throughout. Highly recommended!

—G. B. (Australia)

coming soon

Walk Away Silver Heart

Part 1 of **A Love Poetry Trilogy** is *walk away silver heart*, and features love poems inspired by Amy Lowell's *Madonna of the Evening Flowers*.

Rescue and Redemption

Part 3 of **Part 3** of **A Love Poetry Trilogy** is *rescue and redemption*, and features love poems inspired by T.S. Eliot's *The Love Song of J. Alfred Prufrock*.

FrankPrem.com

www.ingramcontent.com/pod-product-compliance
Lightning Source LLC
Chambersburg PA
CBHW071742080526
44588CB00013B/2131